The Sense of Smell

ELLEN WEISS

Children's Press®
An Imprint of Scholastic Inc.
New York Toronto London Auckland Sydney
Mexico City New Delhi Hong Kong
Danbury, Connecticut

Content Consultant

Lawrence J. Cheskin, M.D.
Johns Hopkins Bloomberg School of Public Health
Baltimore, MD

Library of Congress Cataloging-in-Publication Data

Weiss, Ellen.
  The sense of smell / by Ellen Weiss.
    p. cm. -- (A true book)
  Includes index.
    ISBN-13: 978-0-531-16872-1 (lib. bdg.)
              978-0-531-21834-1 (pbk.)
    ISBN-10: 0-531-16872-7 (lib. bdg.)
              0-531-21834-1 (pbk.)

1. Smell--Juvenile literature. I. Title. II. Series.

  QP458.W385 2008
  612.8'6--dc22   2007048084

Produced by Weldon Owen Education Inc.

1 2 3 4 5 6 7 8 9 10 R 18 17 16 15 14 13 12 11 10 09

Find the Truth!

Everything you are about to read is true *except* for one of the sentences on this page.

Which one is **TRUE**?

T or F Babies don't have a sense of smell until they're eighteen months old.

T or F How something smells to you depends partly on what you think it is.

Find the answers in this book.

Contents

THE BIG TRUTH!

Brain Power

All people except identical twins have their own individual scent.

Our sense of smell helps us balance the ingredients in what we are cooking.

CHAPTER 1

The Forgotten Sense

You're at home when you smell something. It's not a good smell. "Isn't that gas?" you ask. You and your family quickly leave the house. You go to the neighbors' house to phone for help. As you enter, you sniff something mouth-watering. "Mmm, spaghetti sauce—my favorite smell," you think. Imagine that episode without your sense of smell.

The gas in a gas stove has no odor. A special odor is added so that you'll smell a gas leak.

7

Smell for Safety

Like all your senses, smell gives you information about your surroundings. Some people consider smell the least important of the senses. It is sometimes even called the forgotten sense. However, in some parts of the world, smell is greatly admired.

Smell can make your life safer and more pleasurable. If you could not smell, you would not be able to detect leaking gas. You would not know that the milk had gone bad. If you could not smell, you would also miss out on the aroma of baking bread and the smell of summer rain.

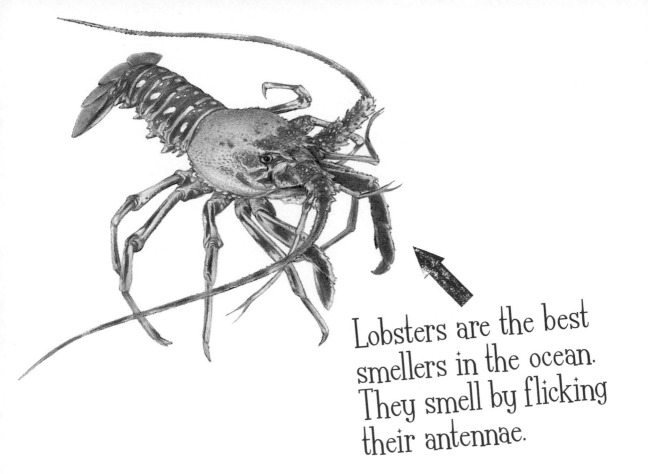

Lobsters are the best smellers in the ocean. They smell by flicking their antennae.

The First Sense

Scientists believe that smell is the most ancient of the senses. The earliest animals on Earth could smell before they could see or hear. These ocean dwellers relied on their sense of smell to alert them to danger. Smell also helped them find food and recognize other animals of their own type.

Smell the Memories

Smell can awaken long-forgotten memories more powerfully than the other four senses can. That is because the pathway for smell messages in the brain is connected to the parts of the brain associated with long-term memory, pleasure, and emotion. A smell often triggers a memory, especially in an older person. The smell of wood smoke might call to mind childhood evenings by the campfire. The memory might include the glow of embers and a chorus of nighttime insects. However, it is the smell that has prompted these images.

A strong smell, like that of wood smoke, can often bring back memories.

I Know You

Before newborn babies can see much of anything, they can distinguish the smell of their mother from the odors of other people. They can do this by the time they are two days old. In the same way, a mother will immediately recognize the scent of her own baby. All this smelling was designed to help our species survive. Mothers and babies need to form bonds. Smell helps them do it.

Females have a better sense
of smell than males do.

CHAPTER 2

Air and Aromas

Your sense of smell is at its best when you are about ten years old.

Because smells enter your nose with the air you breathe, you might think they are some kind of gas. Actually, all odors are made of tiny particles called **molecules**. Molecules are the building blocks of everything around us. Each odor you smell is made of molecules of chemicals.

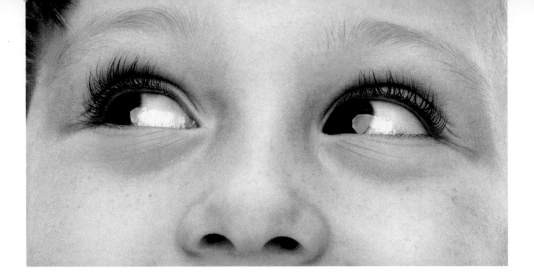

Your nostrils take turns. You breathe through one nostril for three or four hours. Then you switch to the other one.

Nose Jobs

The two jobs of the nose are breathing and smelling. These often happen at the same time, when air passes through the two nostrils, or nasal passages. The nasal passages are lined with **mucus** (MYOO-kuhss). Mucus is important to both breathing and smelling.

When you breathe through your nose, air flows from the nasal passages to the back of the throat and into the lungs. On that same inhalation, odor molecules travel up the nasal passages too. However, these molecules dissolve in the mucus at the very top of the **nasal cavity**. When you eat, odor molecules from your food dissolve there too.

The smell of trash is stronger on hot days. That's because heat increases activity in odor molecules.

The Keys to Smell

At the top of each nasal passage is a patch of mucus-covered skin. The patch is about the size of a postage stamp. Each patch contains about five million **olfactory neurons**, or receptor cells. Each of these cells has tiny hairs, called cilia (SILL-ee-uh). They extend into the nasal passage and "catch" odor molecules.

Receptor cells and odor molecules are like chemical locks and keys. The "lock" of the receptor cell opens only when the right "smell key" comes along. Each receptor cell is built to receive a particular type of odor molecule.

Once a receptor cell has absorbed an odor molecule, it turns it into an electrical signal. The signal travels along the nerve fiber to the **olfactory bulb**. Shaped like a tiny cucumber, the olfactory bulb is actually part of the brain.

The Nose and the Brain

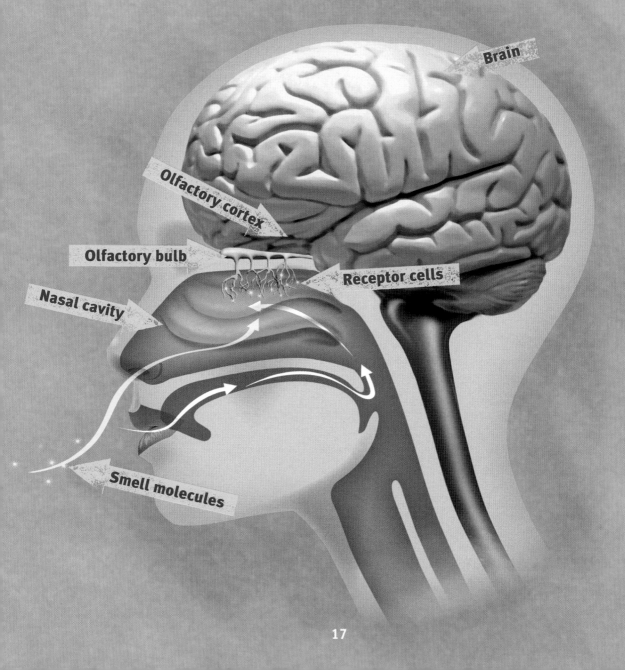

Brain

Olfactory cortex

Olfactory bulb

Receptor cells

Nasal cavity

Smell molecules

A Special Sense

The olfactory bulb is unusual. It sends electrical smell messages straight to the olfactory **cortex**. This is the part of the brain that interprets smells. This route is the most direct of any of the senses.

The smell receptors themselves are also unusual. Each cell lives for about six weeks. The cell then dies off and is replaced. The "new" cell forms exactly behind the "old" cell. Scientists think this may contribute to the long-lasting associations tied to certain smells.

Once we learn a smell, it always smells the same to us, even though we are continually using new receptor cells to smell with.

18

Scent Signals

In order for any of your senses to work, it needs the help of your brain. The brain works with electrical signals. A smell molecule enters the nose as a chemical "message." The olfactory receptors change it to an electrical one and send it to the brain. The brain lets us know what a smell is.

What makes sneakers stink? Sweat from your feet gets into your socks and shoes. Bacteria feed on the sweat and produce a smelly odor.

It also "decides" whether a smell is healthy or unhealthy or whether we've smelled it before. Every day, we take in many more odors than our brains make us aware of.

19

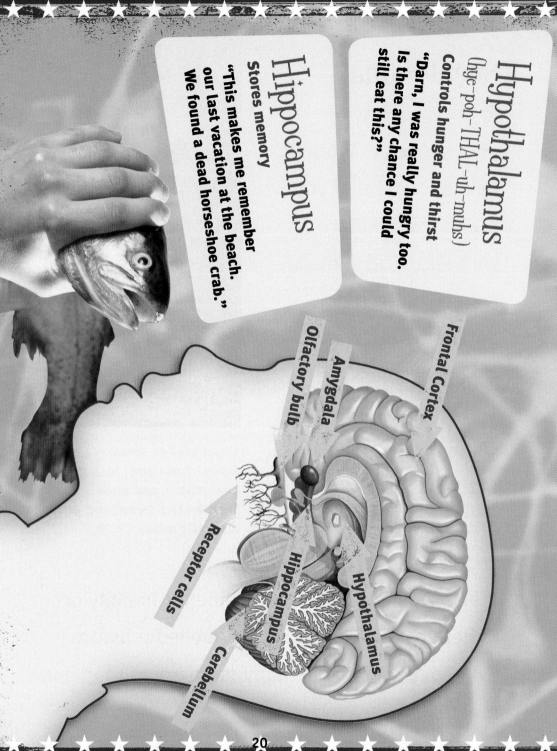

Hypothalamus
(hye-poh-THAL-uh-muhs)

Controls hunger and thirst

"Darn, I was really hungry too. Is there any chance I could still eat this?"

Hippocampus

Stores memory

"This makes me remember our last vacation at the beach. We found a dead horseshoe crab."

Frontal Cortex

Olfactory bulb

Amygdala

Receptor cells

Hippocampus

Hypothalamus

Cerebellum

Brain Power

When you smell, many different parts of the brain are working. These areas control memory, emotions, hunger, and thinking. Other senses do not affect the brain in this way. See what messages are sent to your brain when you smell an old fish.

Amygdala
(uh-MIG-duh-luh)

Controls emotional reactions

"Yuck! Stinky, rotten fish!"

Olfactory Bulb

Controls odor perception

"This fish smells old."

Frontal Cortex

Controls reason and thought

"I wonder how long this fish has been in the fridge? I'd better throw it away right now."

Cerebellum
(ser-uh-BEL-uhm)

Controls movement, balance, and sensory perception

"This looks and smells like a fish."

Simply by smelling fruit, you can often tell if it's ripe or rotten.

CHAPTER 3

The Chemical Senses

Have you noticed that when you have a cold or a blocked nose, food doesn't taste as good? Smell and taste work together to help your brain identify the flavors of food. If we can't smell, it can be difficult to tell the difference between certain foods and drinks. In fact, scientists think that most of what we call "taste" is actually smell!

Our sense of smell is responsible for about 75 percent of what we taste.

Taste Versus Smell

Taste buds on your tongue enable you to taste the four basic flavors—salty, sweet, sour, and bitter. But your ability to distinguish many different smells improves your sense of taste. If you have a very good nose, you can make a living using it. The food industry and manufacturers of perfumes and deodorants hire professional sniffers to test their products and analyze the smells.

A person who tests fragrances for perfume is called a nose.

Fooling Your Nose

Sometimes your nose can be fooled.

How something smells to you depends partly on what you think it is. This was proved by scientists who did an experiment with the smell of cheddar cheese. Some of the people in the experiment were told the smell was cheddar cheese. Another group was given the same thing to smell. But they were told it was body odor. Even though the smell was exactly the same, you can probably guess which group found the smell more agreeable.

The taste of chocolate would not be as strong if you could not smell the chocolate as well.

A sniffer dog can track down a person's unique scent. A dog smells in rapid sniffs to send odor molecules up the nasal passages.

CHAPTER 4

Smelling Well and Smelling Good

Smell has a big effect on how people behave toward each other. Each one of us has our very own "smell fingerprint" that makes us smell unique. Our hands, feet, mouths, underarms, and all our other parts have particular smells.

A dog has more than 200 million receptor cells in its nose. That's about 20 times more than a human.

Personal Scent

Many things go into a person's individual smell. Our diets, our **genes**, our skin color, our hair color, and our age can affect the smell we have. Even our moods, any medication we take, and the weather can change how we smell. Heat makes smell molecules more active. So our body

odor is stronger on a hot day than on a cool day. Friendships and romances have a lot to do with how people smell to each other.

When exercising, sweat makes our body odor stronger. Washing your body daily with soap and water cuts down on sweaty odors. Washing your clothes also helps.

Get Into the Mood

Smell can affect our mood and behavior. Doctors at one hospital found a way to help patients be less anxious about having medical tests. When they piped the smell of vanilla into the room, people were calmer and less worried.

In another experiment, drivers who smelled bad odors, such as exhaust fumes and industrial smoke, became angrier and more short-tempered.

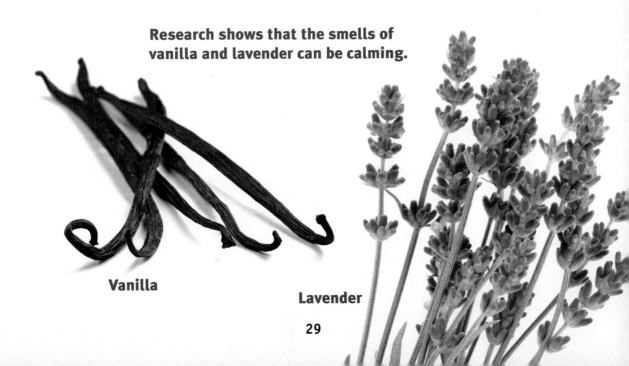

Research shows that the smells of vanilla and lavender can be calming.

Vanilla

Lavender

Chemical Attraction

About 50 years ago, scientists discovered a new set of chemicals among animals. They are called **pheromones** (FEHR-uh-mohnz). Animals give off pheromones to send others of their species messages through scent. When animals are threatened or injured, they release pheromones to warn others. Pheromones are also used to mark territory and to attract other animals.

Artificial pheromones are used to control pests. Crops are sometimes sprayed with pheromones that stop insects from breeding.

Why do we like some people and not others? Scientists say it's because of pheromone scents we give off.

Humans have pheromones too. Men and women give off different kinds of pheromones. Special receptor cells near the entrance of the nose pick up pheromones. The cells send signals to the part of the brain that produces emotion. Pheromones don't have a "smell" that people are aware of. But their effect helps people decide whom they find attractive.

In temples throughout Asia, incense is burned as an offering to ancestors.

CHAPTER 5

Scents Around Us

If you cook with spices, you'll know that some become fragrant when heated. For thousands of years, people all over the world have burned **incense** in ceremonies or for medicinal purposes. Incense powder, sticks, and cones are made from natural materials, such as herbs, barks, seeds, saps, and flowers. They fill the air with pleasant aromas as they burn.

Incense made from citronella is used to repel mosquitoes.

Smells Like Fun

For years, people have been working on ways to use smells to go with movies. In 1916, before movies even had sound, a theater in Pennsylvania tried it. It was for the screening of a film about the Rose Bowl Game. Cotton wool was dipped in rose oil. It was put in front of an electric fan. The smell of roses wafted out into the audience.

Then, in 1939, a scientist tested an invention called Scentovision. It had pipes going to each seat in a theater. Aromas could be sent to viewers at exact times.

Perfume Time Line

3000 B.C.

Ancient Egyptians use incense to perfume the air in ceremonies.

200 B.C.

Ancient Romans use oils made from tree sap and spices on themselves and on pet dogs and cats.

In 1960, a movie called *Scent of Mystery* used a new version of Scentovision called Smell-O-Vision. It was not a hit. The machine made a hissing noise. Some people got too much or too little scent.

A few movie makers have made scratch-and-sniff cards to go with their films. The cards are scratched to release odors during certain scenes. More recently, a company has used Internet technology in a fragrance system for theaters. Devices placed under theater seats are timed to emit scents using information via a Web link.

1000 A.D. ➡ 1656

Persian scientist Avicenna (av-uh-SEN-uh) extracts perfumed oil from a rose flower.

A society of glove and perfume makers is founded in France. Perfumed gloves are all the rage.

How Does It Smell to YOU?

Certain things smell "good" or "bad" to most people. Many think a rose smells sweet, or that skunk spray is stinky. But how something smells depends on the person, as well as social beliefs and behaviors. Strong scents like **musk** were once favored. Today, flowery perfumes are more popular. Scientists have yet to figure out why certain things smell different to different people.

A skunk releases a strong-smelling spray when it is alarmed or threatened.

Skunk spray contains sulfur. It smells like a mix of rotten eggs, garlic, and burned rubber.

Seven Smells

Humans smell seven basic odors that help them detect objects. They are called the primary odors. Professional sniffers must be able to clearly distinguish these smells.

Musky—such as aftershave

Floral

Minty

Ethereal (i-THEER-ee-uhl) —such as cleaning fluid

Pungent (PUHN-juhnt) —such as vinegar

Putrid (PYOO-trid) —such as rotten eggs

Camphoric (kam-FOR-ik) —such as mothballs

When the nose is blocked,
odor molecules cannot
reach the olfactory nerves.

CHAPTER 6

From Nose to Doze

Losing your sense of smell isn't as serious a problem as losing your sight or your hearing. The most common reason for losing the sense of smell is aging. Colds or allergies may block your nose from time to time. Brain injuries or nervous disorders can also affect the sense of smell. The loss of the ability to smell is called anosmia (an-OZ-mee-uh).

← Anosmia can be either temporary or permanent.

Answers to Anosmia

Some people are born with anosmia. It may run in the family. It is not life-threatening. However, it does affect the quality of a person's life. There is no single cure for anosmia. Drugs, herbs, or surgery may help restore the sense of smell. Sometimes people with anosmia can detect odors such as harmful chemicals. This is because some "bad" smells actually stimulate pain receptors, rather than olfactory ones!

Your sense of smell is weak in the morning. It gets better as the day goes on.

If you can't smell burning toast, it may be because your sense of smell hasn't woken up properly!

Tired Nose

Sometimes your nose just gets tired. This condition is called "olfactory fatigue." Have you ever noticed that, after smelling the same smell for an hour or two, you can't really smell it any more? That's because receptor cells get less sensitive after a while. It happens even if the smell is awful. That's good news for people who work in stinky places!

The stench of a fish market may be unbearable at first. However, after a while, the nose gets used to the smell.

Be Nice to Your Nose

Luckily, you don't have to be as careful about damaging your sense of smell as you do about damaging your hearing or your sight. However, it pays to sniff unfamiliar things with caution. Inhaling strong chemicals and gas odors can cause a loss of smell. A safer way is to use your hand to wave the scent of a chemical gently toward your nose. Be nice to your nose and your sense of smell will serve you well. ★

"Stop and smell the roses" is a saying that means "slow down and enjoy life."

True Statistics

Speed of air entering the nose when you inhale:
4 miles (6.4 kilometers) per hour

Speed of air entering the nose when you sniff:
20 miles (32 kilometers) per hour

Number of smell molecules needed to produce an impulse in an olfactory neuron: 8

Number of olfactory neurons that must be stimulated before we smell something: 40

How accurate our memory of smell is after one year: About 65 percent

Number of people in the United States that suffer from anosmia: Two to five million

Did you find the truth?

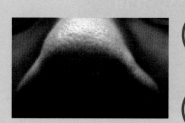

F Babies don't have a sense of smell until they're eighteen months old.

T How something smells to you depends partly on what you think it is.

Resources

Books

Artell, Mike. *Pee-Yew!: The Stinkiest, Smelliest Animals, Insects, and Plants on Earth!* Minneapolis: Tandem Library, 2005.

Cobb, Vicki. *Follow Your Nose: Discover Your Sense of Smell*. Brookfield, CT: Millbrook Press, 2003.

Hickman, Pamela. *Animal Senses: How Animals See, Hear, Taste, Smell, and Feel* (Animal Behavior). Toronto: Kids Can Press, 1998.

Pringle, Laurence P. *Smell* (Explore Your Senses). New York: Benchmark Books, 1999.

Pryor, Kimberley Jane. *Smelling* (Senses). New York: Chelsea Clubhouse, 2003.

Ripoll, Jaime. *How Our Senses Work* (Invisible World). New York: Chelsea House Publishers, 1995.

Silverstein, Alvin. *Smelling and Tasting* (Senses and Sensors). Brookfield, CT: Twenty-First Century Books, 2002.

Taylor-Butler, Christine. *The Respiratory System* (A True Book: Health and the Human Body). Danbury, CT: Children's Press, 2008.

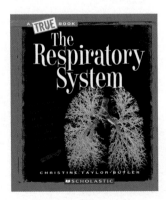

Organizations and Web Sites

Neuroscience for Kids

http://faculty.washington.edu/chudler/nosek.html

Learn about the olfactory system, then try some smell experiments.

What the Nose Knows

www.riverdeep.net/current/2002/01/012102_nose.jhtml

Find out how humans and other animals smell.

Sense of Smell Institute

www.senseofsmell.org/feature/smell101/index.php

Get more detailed information from the Smell 101 lessons on this advanced Web site.

Places to Visit

Science Museum of Virginia

2500 West Broad Street
Richmond, VA 23220-2057
(804) 864 1400
www.smv.org/nowshowing/
exhibitions/bioscape.asp
Test your senses in the
My Size Gallery.

International Perfume Museum

8 Place du Cours
06130 Grasse
France
+33 (4) 9705 5800
www.museesdegrasse.com/
MIP/fla_ang/mip_accueil_html.
shtml
See how perfume was made
through the ages.

Important Words

bacteria (bak-TIHR-ee-uh) – tiny living things too small to be seen without a microscope

cortex – the outer layer of an internal organ such as the brain

gene – the part of a cell that controls how a living thing looks and develops

incense – a substance that is burned for its aroma

molecule (MOL-uh-kyool) – the smallest particle into which a substance can be divided while remaining the same substance

mucus (MYOO-kuhss) – a slimy fluid that protects the breathing passages

musk – a strong-smelling substance secreted by some animals

nasal cavity – the open area inside and behind the nose

olfactory bulb – one of two bulb-like parts of the brain that connect to the olfactory nerves

olfactory neuron – a cell that receives information from odor molecules and sends that information to the brain in the form of electrical signals

pheromone (FEHR-uh-mohn) – a chemical substance released by an animal which sends a message to others of the same species

Index

Page numbers in **bold** indicate illustrations.

About the Author

Ellen Weiss went to Oberlin College and Columbia University, and she likes to remember how the coffee smelled in the snack bar at Oberlin. She has written over 200 books, fiction and nonfiction, for children of all ages, as well as songs and videos for kids. Her work has won a Grammy Award, a Parents' Choice Award, and three Children's Choice Awards. She and her husband, Mel Friedman, live in New York City. They often collaborate on books. The Disney Channel adapted one of their books, *The Poof Point*, for a television movie.

PHOTOGRAPHS: Big Stock Photo (pp. 3–4; pp. 7–8; p. 25; p. 29; © Larry Jordan, p. 30; p. 33; p. 36; aftershave, vinegar, p. 37; p. 40; p. 43); Digital Vision (p. 14); Getty Images (p. 22; p. 32; gloves, p. 35; p. 42); Ingram Image Library (back cover); iStockphoto.com (© Michal Herman, strawberries, p. 5; © Nathan Maxfield, front cover; © Yvonne Chamberlain, twins, p. 5; © Lisa F. Young, p. 31); Photo New Zealand (age fotostock/© Patrick Luethy, p. 18; age fotostock/© Targa, p. 24; topfoto, Egyptian incense, p. 34); Photodisc (rose, p. 35); Photolibrary (p. 6; p. 10; p. 12; p. 15; p. 26; p. 34; p. 41); Stock.Xchng (spray, flower, mint, egg, p. 37); Tranz/Corbis (p. 11; pp. 19–20; p. 28; p. 38)